The
BOOMER'S
GUIDE *to a*

WORRY-FREE
RETIREMENT

THE
BOOMER'S
GUIDE *to a*
WORRY-FREE
RETIREMENT

SLEEP-WELL
INVESTMENT
STRATEGIES

Thomas F. Helbig

Published by Advantage, Charleston, South Carolina.
Member of Advantage Media Group.

ADVANTAGE is a registered trademark and the Advantage colophon is a trademark of Advantage Media Group, Inc.

Printed in the United States of America.

ISBN: 978-159932-293-3
LCCN: 2012935977

This publication is designed to provide accurate and authoritative information in regard to the subject matter covered. It is sold with the understanding that the publisher is not engaged in rendering legal, accounting, or other professional services. If legal advice or other expert assistance is required, the services of a competent professional person should be sought.

Advantage Media Group is proud to be a part of the Tree Neutral® program. Tree Neutral offsets the number of trees consumed in the production and printing of this book by taking proactive steps such as planting trees in direct proportion to the number of trees used to print books. To learn more about Tree Neutral, please visit www.treeneutral.com. To learn more about Advantage's commitment to being a responsible steward of the environment, please visit www.advantagefamily.com/green

Advantage Media Group is a leading publisher of business, motivation, and self-help authors. Do you have a manuscript or book idea that you would like to have considered for publication? Please visit www.amgbook.com or call 1.866.775.1696

TABLE OF CONTENTS

Introduction

L ike any author, I am publishing this book in the hope that you will enjoy reading it and absorb valuable information from it. I feel strongly about what's expressed in these pages and truly believe that it will help you make sound investment decisions.

I've been in the financial services industry since 1977, witnessing profound changes in the financial markets and in our economy during that time. What you will find in these pages are ideas and observations from my 35 years as an advisor working only with retirees and those about to retire. Because I work with that age group, I have always leaned toward safety and away from risk.

In the early part of my career, when aggressive portfolios were being rewarded, I still favored conservative investing. That was how I structured my own attempts to build wealth, and I extended it to my clients. As time has passed, my thinking has come to match the needs of the times. Or maybe the times have come to match my thinking. I wish the cause of that gradual change was something other than losses and reversals for the average investor, but the losses have been extensive for most portfolios—there is no denying it.

Capitalism is a powerful, proven engine, and the American version of it is highly dynamic. The world's most envied economy with its competitive and innovative ways is a place where intelligent investors can and should profit. That's simple logic. Businesses need up-front investment to grow, and our capital markets are designed to provide it. If average citizens choose to participate in that process, they would logically stand a good chance of sharing in the profits that are generated—through appreciation of share prices, or dividends, or both. History shows that certain stars must align for this to happen—and right now the stars are having great trouble lining up properly. America's financial system is in very shaky condition, like others around the world.

More and more people have lost trust in what was once a reasonably reliable wealth-builder, the U.S. stock market. Average investors lack faith in the equities market now. They are weary of the collapses and afraid of future calamities. They don't know where to turn, and it is widely believed that the bull markets of the 1980s and '90s are in the past and not to be repeated any time in the near or not-so-near future. "We're in a whole new normal," I've heard many say, and by all means I agree.

While this attitude shift has occurred, safety-minded advisors like me have been given new tools to work with. What I'm able to offer, by way of investment vehicles that are safe but potentially very profitable, has increased significantly. I appreciate the position I'm in and the value I'm able to offer to my clients.

This book is written to benefit retirees and people in the preretirement stage. Much of what is presented in the book will be of value to workers in their 30s or 40s who happen to be very farsighted and future-oriented, but mainly it is for people at the far end of their careers, or who are finished working.

I'm not certain if this book will earn a prime spot in the financial section of your bookshelves, but I do hope it does. I am not a born writer, but my thoughts were clear in mind and my beliefs were well-formed when I sat down to gather this material. I believe strongly in all the statements you'll be reading.

In addition, my thoughts in writing this book have the clarity of someone who comes to the task well-rested. By that, I mean that I sleep well at night. I may be a financial advisor operating in extremely volatile times, but I don't toss and turn, because I know my clients' funds are well-protected. In this business, you could find yourself staring at the ceiling, expecting phone calls the next day from clients panicked about the stock market collapsing. I don't get those calls. What I get are calls of appreciation. It's a great feeling when the person on the other end of the phone is saying: "Thank you for protecting my money the way you did, because when the market plunged, I had no losses and no anxiety." To me, a message like that is more rewarding than any other.

Retirement
Advisory
Group

To learn more about safe retirement strategies, please call **Thomas Helbig** at **314-993-9494**, or email him at **thomas@retirementkey.com.**

Visit **www.retirementkey.com** for information on seminars, workshops and services.

Chapter 1

INVESTMENT REALITY VS. WISHFUL THINKING

chapter one

I n a free-market economy, with all the advantages conveyed by a society like America's, with our history of success and global leadership, does the value of our publicly traded companies trend upward naturally and inevitably?

That's a question worth asking.

In the great market crash of 1929, fortunes were lost. By July of 1932, the U.S. stock market had lost 89 percent of its pre-crash value. That was the low point—rock bottom. It's always good to "find a bottom," as the stock market analysts say, because the direction you go from there is up, and up is good.

What people don't realize is how long an upward climb our stock market had to endure. From that day in 1929, it took a generation—all the way to 1954—for the market to recover, for the Dow Jones Industrial Average just to break even with the level it was at the day before the big crash. That was the worst economic period of all, the great market crash, followed by the Great Depression. All in all, we had about 25 long, tough years to reach our pre-crash stock valuations.

Let's think about the person who entered the workforce sometime not long after that 1954 point when stock prices pulled even with pre-crash prices. I've worked with many people from this post-World War II generation. They had enhanced education opportunities through the G.I. Bill of Rights. They were part of an expanding economy. They had a well-established work ethic—part of the culture they grew up in. They knew all about collapse and scarcity, but they were in a good position because we had recovery by the time they were into their careers. They were the parents of the baby boom generation, in their prime after World War II, when industries were building and the capital markets were moving upward.

The parents of the boomers had an experience that was marked by an expanding economy and the chance to invest in solid growth stocks. That scenario had a stability to it that led to a sense of permanent, ongoing prosperity and bullish investment attitudes. It painted a picture, one that has hung around a lot longer than it deserved to. People today have a wrong impression of the equity markets, of the basic nature of them, but that's fairly understandable, because the impression in their minds did hold true for quite a while. The market went up during the 1950s and '60s. The middle class expanded. Those were prosperous times, for solid, fundamental reasons.

The market went up again during the 1980s and 1990s, but that was more of a bubble economy, with cheap credit and so-called "irrational exuberance" fueling economic growth. Still, it was another period that contributed to the idea that the stock market naturally goes up, and the down periods are just temporary exceptions.

It is so often said that the long-term investor enjoys powerful advantages over the speculator, over the stock player who is trying to snatch up profits in a tight time frame. The person who is in it for the long haul can ride out the down markets. He can take advantage of the fact that the U.S. is a dynamic growth economy. He can be part of that rising tide that, eventually, lifts all boats.

Those are nice words, but to my view they make the investment challenge sound considerably simpler and easier than it really is. It truly is harder to capture a respectable return on a consistent basis than some would suggest. At the end of 1964, the Dow Jones Industrial Average stood at 874 points. Fast-forward 17 years, to the end of 1981, and we see the Dow Industrials at 875 points. Those 17 years cover three recessions and three periods of expansion. They include the Vietnam War, the first moon walk and the Watergate scandal. For the average person who works, saves and invests, those 17 years cover about one half of the time that they are trying to build wealth. What was the per-year gain from 1964 through '81? Well, it was essentially nothing, but to give it an exact percentage it was .007. Just like James Bond, only with a decimal point in front of it.

I can take this point about long-term investing a step further. Imagine that such long dry spells didn't exist in the U.S. equity markets. Let's assume that, while there is volatility—there are some dramatic spikes—there aren't the long, dormant periods without an upward tilt. Under that scenario, a buy-and-hold investor would have to worry about losing a decade or wasting 17 years as the markets zig, zag and eventually go nowhere. That investor, if his goal is to build a solid, substantial retirement account, is still playing Russian roulette. Depending on when he retires, he could take one last beating that dramatically reduces his quality of life over the next 15 to 25 years.

Think about this: Executive A and Executive B have the same amount of money in their retirement accounts, only they were born a year apart. Executive A retires one year and Executive B retires the following year. The year that Mr. A retires, a fairly lengthy bull market is in its final push, and so Mr. A rides that out, leaves the workplace and tells his broker to convert all his holdings to cash. Mr. B decides he'll do the same, when his turn comes. Except the market falls off a cliff during that last year.

And wouldn't you know, Mr. B is retiring on maybe 40 percent less than Mr. A.

Most of us have received a heavy dose of Wall Street wisdom over the past 30 or 40 years, telling us that the first rule of financial planning is 'safety through diversification." What I want to explain is what real diversification is. When you are diversified on Wall Street, you can invest in small-cap stocks, mid-cap stocks, large-cap stocks, international stocks, specific industries and sectors, or you can invest in exchange-traded funds (ETFs), bonds, or mutual funds. Every one of these is registered as a security. That's a funny word for it, "security," because the one universal trait of securities is risk. Meaning, you could lose what you invest. Still, what we're told by Wall Street is that some of this type of risk plus some of that type of risk, plus a little of this other type of risk, adds up to greatly reduced risk. What investor hasn't been told: "As long as you diversify among all those securities, you'll be all right."

That's where I, as a financial advisor, stop and ask: "Is this true diversification?" Every one of those securities I just listed is subject to market fluctuation. They're all subject to political uncertainty; they're all subject to the reality of terrorism, among other extreme possibilities. If you travel by air, you know that it was a lot easier to get on a plane before September 2001 than it is today. To my view, the need for air-travel security is matched by a new need for caution on the part of investors. Wall Street will tell you not to put all your eggs in one basket, but the seemingly different baskets that Wall Street offers are not really so. Diversify the way the securities industry suggests, and in my view you're not truly diversified.

Diversification, asset allocation, and a long-term outlook—these are strategies we've been offered. Yes, they can help to reduce risk when investing in equities, but by no means do they come close to eliminating it. When describing the long-term perspective or strategy, many a Wall Street advisor will boil that down to "buy and hold." Pick a well-managed fund or a basket of blue chip stocks, purchase your shares, and stay the course. You won't be able to time the market ups and downs, but over the long term America grows, good companies make profits, and they may even pay dividends, so be patient.

If there is a possibility of losing money, we're talking speculation, not investment. There are no guarantees that stocks will offer profitable returns in the future, even in the long run. It only takes one gigantic loss to collapse a dream. Many ordinary Americans trusted in Enron and WorldCom with their retirement dreams, and they ended up with a nightmare. Though most advisors and brokers have been saying "buy-and-hold" for the last 30 or 40 years, this strategy only benefits Wall Street.

What you have to start asking is "hold until when?" At some point, you must make your exit. Therefore it is vital that you possess, throughout your risk-tolerant years, an exit strategy. Buy-and-hold only works in a bull market. The buy-and-hold strategy fails in a flat or down market. I think back to an article I saw not long ago in Money Magazine. It points out how, over the last 40-plus years, it's been so easy for an advisor to just buy and hold. Brokers usually average about 2 percent a year in commissions, and by telling an investor to just buy and hold, they get the highest commissions by doing absolutely nothing.

It takes a lot more work for a broker or advisor to practice asset allocation, watching the markets and the account-holder's retirement account and constantly changing it based on market fluctuations. It's so much easier for a broker to just say "buy-and-hold." You're riding a roller-coaster, and the broker keeps getting the fees.

The close cousin of buy-and-hold is a technique called dollar cost averaging. On paper, it makes tremendous sense. Here is how it works. Basically you are feeding money into a fund or account on a very regular, very scheduled basis. Investors do this when they are in their peak earning years. They designate a certain sum of money to come out of their paycheck, so that they are contributing every week or every other week or perhaps every month into their retirement account.

Here's how dollar cost averaging works: When you're putting money in, even when the market is going down, you're still buying shares at a lower cost. Even though you're losing money, your money's still going into your account. You are buying shares at a lower cost. And so you are making 12 or 24 purchases in a year on a scheduled basis. If the market goes down, the cost of that share is less, so you're buying at a lower cost, and you're getting more shares. For example, if you are buying ABCD Mid-Cap Fund this way, you may be looking at the net asset value (NAV) of the fund on the 20th of the month, noticing that it is $8.25 a share. You look again on the 28th of the month and it's up to $8.40 a share, so you're happy. However on the 31st the price falls, down to $8.10. On one hand, you're disappointed, but since your automatic purchase happens on the first of the next month, you know that the funds taken from your paycheck will be purchasing a greater number of shares at $8.10 than at $8.25 or $8.40. So, you end up with those extra shares, through the machinery of dollar-cost averaging, and you simply root for the NAV to trend upward again.

We had a 20-year bull market during the 1980s and '90s. Twenty years is the longest bull market our nation has ever seen, so most people of a certain generation are accustomed to very positive thinking. They walk around thinking: "This is the only way to make money, the market always goes up." Well, for those 20 years it did—again, driven by "bubble" factors like very easy credit. Once 2000 hit, that all ended. We had a bear market from 2000 to 2002 and then another bear market in '08, and look at where we are now.

As I write this book, we are at levels from 1999, so we've had a flat market. Anyone who followed the buy-and-hold strategy in that era was left high and dry. They basically went backward because taxes and inflation never stopped over those 12 years. On September 13, 1999, the Dow Jones Industrial Average closed at 11,030. Fast forward to September 12, 2011, and you will note that the DJIA closed at 11,061. That's 12 years of no growth, nothing to show for it. Not on a cumulative basis, anyway. In other words, if you look at the index graph, left to right on the page, you won't see a constantly rising line. Not to say there weren't lots of gains, but my question to a prospective client who has been in the market with his retirement portfolio is this: Did you capture those gains?

How do you capture a gain? The only way you capture a gain is by selling, so if you just rode that roller-coaster of buy-and-hold, and you never really sold anything, you didn't gain anything. You were up, you were down, you've made money, you gave it back, you made gains, you gave it back, you made gains, you gave it back, and that's what most people do, and they don't realize it until it's too late. We've had a lost decade.

Even if a broker does advise you to sell, it tends very often to be a sale of one equity asset and purchase of another. They'll very rarely tell you, "Get out of stocks into cash," because once it goes into cash that is not money under management, and then that broker gets no fees or loads or commissions. When I say cash, I'm talking about safe investments.

The brokerage business has a model, and you can see it in action. Mutual fund shares are what most IRA and 401(k) accounts invest in. If you read the prospectus they send you, or ask enough questions, you will have no illusions about the fact that there are big expenses to cover. There's the cost of the money manager, the advertising, the broker and other marketing and sales support. Fees, some of which are called loads, have to be charged. You can choose to pay your load in various ways, with some chance of getting certain load charges waived if you hold the shares long enough. You could purchase Class A shares, and pay the load up front, or choose Class B shares and pay when you redeem, or sell, the shares. In some cases those Class B shares will convert to Class A, meaning you have held them long enough that there won't be a charge when you redeem. But all that means is that you've sat there long enough kicking in your annual maintenance fee and expense cost that the fund company is willing to give you a break on the load.

I teach a lot of educational workshops for the public. A few people at my workshops are active day traders. That's their hobby and they love it and enjoy the thrill of it, but they're constantly on their computers. They buy low and they sell high, and they do okay. They even do well avoiding fees. If you are a day trader, conducting transactions online using a company like

Ameritrade or eTrade, you can do that without getting hit with significant fees. That's quite interesting, because your account is so active in that situation. When you're like most people in the world of buy-and-hold, your account is quite passive, but there are still significant, regular fees imposed, around two percent a year. Wall Street is going to get fees from you on your retirement accounts for the rest of your life, and that can add up to a lot of unnecessary costs.

That two percent a year is coming out whether you make money or lose money. In a year like 2008, with so many long down periods, you could be sliding down with your account value and it doesn't matter – Wall Street is still getting paid its two percent. Granted, you do get the service of brokering trades and registering transactions, but most people are not into buying and doing all these trades. It's too much work for a broker to be looking at every individual plan and constantly trading and doing asset allocation. The brokerage reps can't keep up with it, especially the more and more clients they get, so they just ride it out until a client calls in and says, "Hey, let's make a change or something." "Okay, well maybe we'll do a change," the rep responds, but in the meantime he's getting two percent by doing nothing.

On occasions when the broker does call to recommend something, it's often because it represents a payout to the broker of three or four percent instead of two. That's because his firm gets a bonus for selling certain funds or stocks. There are incentives to the brokers, such as trips and cruises. In a given month, they get a fund to push, whether it's the best or not, and that's their job. They push, and the firm gets kickbacks.

For example, all the brokers might get a round-trip ticket if together they sell a couple hundred million dollars worth of a certain mutual fund. So you get a phone call from the portfolio advisor who is trying to win a cruise. He touts the ABCXYZ Consolidated Mutual Fund. "This is a good fund because the guy who's managing it is a really smart guy," he's likely to say. "He's phenomenal, and this is the next up-and-coming fund."

The way Wall Street people and the brokerage companies see the world, this all makes sense. That's because it has been profitable for them over years and decades. Along the way, some individual investors have done quite well. In my view, they are the minority. They have beaten the odds. As an investor, you want much better odds than Wall Street products provide. If you are near or at retirement, you need some strong, enduring guarantees, which is what my advisory practice provides.

Chapter 2

WHEN YOU'RE NO LONGER ACCUMULATING, YOU'RE PRESERVING

---

chapter two

n my practice, I come in contact with many older people whose assets are exposed to an alarmingly high amount of market risk. If you're wondering how much a retiree should have at risk, go by the Rule of 100. Take your age and subtract it from 100. If you're 65 years old, subtract that from 100 and you get 35. So, 35 is the maximum percentage of your portfolio that you should have at risk. Conversely, 65 percent is the share of your retirement money that should have safety and guarantees, and no risk.

That's called the Rule of 100. An 80-year-old should have 80 percent green money—we call that green money, money that's safe—and only 20 percent at risk. The older you get, the more conservative you need to be because if you have too much at risk and the market tanks, you're wiped out. It may not come back in your lifetime.

Many people whom I talk to about the Rule of 100 will think a minute and very likely knit their brow. If they are dealing with a brokerage firm, which nine out of ten of them are, the Rule of 100 is a foreign concept to them. Wall Street doesn't follow this Rule of 100. You know why? Wall Street people only make money if your money is at risk. That's how they get paid. They don't get anything if they have your money in a safe spot; there are no fees available to them for doing that. The broker could sell you a Treasury note or very safe bond, and some of them will do that, but in my experience, the majority of your money is going to be in equities, mutual funds and stocks.

After we've talked about the Rule of 100, I will generally sit down with a prospective client, and we'll recognize that the client's portfolio is upside down. Just as it's bad to be upside down in your mortgage, it's not good to be upside down in your portfolio of retirement-fund holdings. We use a color-coding system to determine this. What percentage is red money, or money at risk? What percentage is green, safe money? When I look at the portfolios of most people who come in to see me, they have at least 90 to 100 percent in red money, and maybe 0 to 10 percent in green money. That's completely upside down, and my job, as an independent advisor, is to get them closer to a position of safety.

Investment advice that gets handed out on television or in Sunday newspaper articles is generally aimed at investors in their active earning years, who therefore are more risk-tolerant. That is easier advice to dish out to an audience of people who can take some risk and who would be able to recover from setbacks and negative years.

However, I work primarily with pre-retirees or retirees. My clients are just about ready to retire or they're already retired, and for them the buy-and-hold strategy in equities does not work anymore. For one thing, they don't have that salary that supports a dollar-cost-averaging program. In general, they aren't risk-tolerant anymore, whether they realize it or not.

In fact, when a retiree begins to use his or her retirement account as intended, and that account is mainly securities— which means that the nest egg is exposed to downside risk— they are in a situation called "reverse dollar-cost averaging." If you retire and stop feeding that retirement account and instead draw income from it as it declines in a down market, you will experience the principle of reverse dollar-cost averaging. Not only is the market going down, you're drawing money out, so you're actually taking more principal out just to keep that same income level. If you're drawing 6 percent and the market's going down 10, you're losing principal, so you need to take more out to keep that 6 percent income flow coming. That's called reverse dollar-cost averaging. It's something the marketing people and sales reps on Wall Street don't tell you about.

That's the situation if your portfolio continues to contain equity holdings. That's what happens if you continue with the approach you used during your income-earning years, even though you have stopped working. You may not actually be buying any more equities, but your money remains tied up in the equities you purchased when you were risk-tolerant.

Most people who have all or most of their money in their 401(k) by definition have their money exposed to the everyday Wall Street risk of the up-down markets. About 80 to 90 percent of retirement accounts that I see have the majority of their investments in equities on Wall Street because that's where the 401(k)s were.

In some ways, I can't blame people for drifting out of the workforce into retirement with a portfolio that looks like a working person's portfolio. That's where they've been for the last 30 and 40 years. That's all they know. In order for people to be a little bit sharper and more aware, they need an exit interview— not as an employee, but as an investor. They need someone to say: "Look, you are on your way out the door, and you should think about this 401(k) account. Changes might be in order."

If you have a 401(k), you really don't have your own advisors. You may have a person from the 401 company come out once a year and say, "You know, if anybody needs any help we'll answer questions," but that's it. That's not financial advice. If workers with 401(k) accounts think that a once-a-year visit and a few remarks are sufficient, that's unfortunate. Most 401(k) plans are with the big mutual fund companies such as Fidelity and Vanguard. Remember, these are Wall Street firms that basically sell mutual funds. When you retire, they still want to control and manage your accounts even when you roll your 401(k) plan into an IRA. So even though you have retired and your risk tolerance should have changed, the broker at these firms basically just kept your assets allocated the way they were when you were working.

I'll go back to my earlier comment about history, about long-term market performance, and about your own personal context as an investor. Not only do your needs and requirements change as you move toward retirement, the investing landscape changes as well. Things happen that strongly suggest we should change our expectations about return on investment in the period ahead. But people have trouble doing that. Whatever market performance they have experienced during their prime years of earning income, raising kids, paying off a home, talking to the neighbor over the fence—that's the market activity or performance that they tend to regard as "normal."

My message to new clients, most of whom still have their wagons hitched to the old ideas of buy-and-hold and diversify among securities, is a simple one. I tell them: "There is no free lunch on Wall Street. If you are a conservative investor, you must avoid individual stocks and equity mutual funds. It's of the utmost importance to protect your principal while earning a return on your investment. If your principal is at risk, you are not an investor, you are gambler. Think about that for a minute. Would you gamble your life savings in Las Vegas?"

I ask that question rhetorically, but I meet with retirees who have 90 percent or more of their life savings at risk on Wall Street. Over my 35 years in this business, I would estimate that of the people who come to my office, 98 percent of them have most of their assets at risk on Wall Street.

Here is a test concerning buy-and-hold as a strategy. This test is for anyone who has ever owned a stock or a mutual fund that had the possibility of going down in price—which is all of them, of course. A high point in the market was October 9, 2007. When the market started heading down, it didn't take a rocket scientist to figure out, even within a few months, that we were in a bear market. Tell me if your advisor or brokerage rep called you and said this: "Okay, it's obvious that we're in a bear market, so it's time to get out. It's time to save ourselves from any more losses."

I have asked that question dozens and dozens of times, and the answer is always the same. Mostly the response comes in the form of silence. The typical investor never got that phone call.

The prospect of an exit basically never comes up, either when the market is peaking or when it's trending down.

Instead, it's just buy and hold. You're riding a roller-coaster, and you just hope you don't get derailed at the bottom as your working days are ending. You cross your fingers that the market will be doing well when you need your money at retirement. Investors experience gains on their stocks and mutual funds, and then if they aren't market-timers, if they consider themselves long-term participants and not prone to speculation, they "let it ride," as they say in the casinos. Those Wall Street gains aren't really your gains if you stay in the market. It's like playing the tables in Las Vegas, and seeing your stack of chips get taller. Those are not your chips until you take them off the game table. If your money is in Wall Street, that's not your money till you get it out of the market.

That's a dangerous game to play with your life savings. If you lose a round, you won't have time to keep your money in play to recover it, the way you could when you were working and had that paycheck coming in and years ahead of you.

Once you retire, you're in a whole new stage of life. It's called the preservation stage. You have to preserve your nest egg, because if you lose it, the game's over. Advisors don't call retirees to urge them to capture their gains, and so they continue to buy and hold. They experience gains on paper, then give them back, and the cycle continues. That's because they aren't selling.

The way to make money in the markets is to buy low and sell high, but most people are not sitting in front of their computer all day long and trading. For one thing, day trading is loaded with risk. And retirees have plenty else to do. They're traveling, they're seeing their grandkids, they're enjoying their retirement years—and meanwhile, they just hope the market goes up. That's the most foolish thing you can do with your retirement account, and that's why I try to educate people to think differently once they're in this new stage of life.

If you can accept the risk of day trading, you can try to make money on the basis of "buy low, sell high." You'll have a chance of coming out ahead. But really, who has time to do that? Now is the time when you have to find alternative investments that you can count on that have guarantees. If you're going to leave your money with Wall Street, you might as well go down to the casino and have fun with it.

I have been consulted by so many people who were getting ready to retire around 2000, when the market crashed, especially the technology stocks that formed the "dot-com bubble." If you had a lot of your portfolio in tech stocks and sold them that February so you could have retirement security, you would have been fortunate. You would have sold near the NASDAQ

Composite peak of 5,132 and really been ahead of the game. Someone else who followed the same strategy but was due to retire a year later, after the NASDAQ had crashed and burned at less than 2,500, would have been in quite the opposite situation. People I met would say to me that they had lost 40 to 50 percent of their life savings and no longer could afford to retire.

If you think of your career as a long plane flight, you can picture the points in time that for you represent taxi-and-take-off, the climb, the cruising altitude (with some turbulence here and there), and then the point of initial descent, followed by a gradual descent, landing, and finally arrival at the gate.

If at all possible, I would like to get started with a client at or before the point where he or she is beginning that "initial descent." There are lots of options we can discuss in early meetings with people who are in their later 50s, or right at age 60. Recently a couple came in to talk to me, and they were not corner-office CEO types by any means but they had done pretty well in their careers. They were both about 60 years old and were gainfully employed. Their comment to me was: "We're going to work until about age 63, and we want to get started now and work with you and get our retirement accounts protected from loss before we actually quit our jobs."

"That's great," I tell people in situations like that. "Let's get started." Just like the pilot of that plane, I have one absolute priority, which is safety—only in my case, it's financial safety. Together we will decide what portion of their current assets should be put aside and no longer subjected to risk. Just because it is protected from risk doesn't mean it's banished to an account that will earn little or nothing, given the interest rate trends.

We get second opinions on our health, so doesn't it make sense that we get a second opinion on our wealth? Most of these people have been saving their whole lives. They've been working with a brokerage firm, and as a result their 401(k) or IRA is fully invested in stocks or mutual funds. No one has ever talked to them about risk reduction or the Rule of 100. Once they see the reality of the situation, they begin to think: This is my net worth, and I need to protect and preserve this to make it last the rest of my life.

I should repeat: The Rule of 100 is critical to understand, but it's a guideline, not an absolute blueprint. Every individual has his or her own comfortable risk tolerance. Discussing this with an advisor is the only way to establish priorities.

There was a time not all that long ago when people might have done a good job of keeping their invested portfolio away from downside risk, yet still incurred the risk that comes with decreased purchasing power. The source of that was price inflation, and it was considerable. Their monthly check would come and it would be the same amount as the month before, but meanwhile everything at the supermarket was a little more than it was the last time they went shopping.

It's natural to be concerned that your funds in retirement are losing some of their purchasing power. A good financial plan will address that. In my approach, we talk about the various worlds where dollars can go to get invested. I show clients what is out there in safe-money places. The tiny amount of interest paid on certificates of deposit, which has been at or less than one percent, doesn't keep up with inflation. But there are other hybrid accounts that not only provide safety and guarantees but also give you above-average returns. In the next chapters I will address these types of accounts—the safe vehicles in which I, and hundreds of my clients, keep our money and life savings.

Chapter 3

HOW INVESTMENT TOOLS FOR RETIREMENT CAME TO BE

chapter three

Before there were 401(k) plans, many corporate and government retirement plans were based on defined-benefit pension plans. These plans were provided by employers, who offered a portion of the worker's annual compensation in the form of a contribution to the pension. Once the pension was fully funded and the employee fully vested, an insurance company would handle the actual maintenance of the account and payout of the income.

Where a pension system breaks down is in the period before the employee retires. The company he works for is saying all the right things about setting aside a percentage of its profits to handle this future liability. When the company lives up to what it's saying, it's a happy ending. When it doesn't, it's quite a tragic ending. This can occur with private-sector companies, and it can also occur with municipalities and government entities.

Most of the old pensions worked out well. But pension plans are set up when sales and profits are strong. When sales and profits decline or disappear, the plans are very difficult to fund. Old-fashioned pensions, known as defined-benefit pensions, came into vogue during the postwar boom and helped big corporations retain valued employees. Over time, however, such plans lost their appeal to the big private-sector employers.

Even the solid-gold, defined-benefit pensions had a major drawback, one that people tended to lose sight of. A classic pension is paid out in full to the retiree for his or her lifetime. In most cases, once that pensioner has died, a monthly sum equal to about half the original amount then will be paid to the surviving spouse. If both die together in a car crash, that's it for the pension—even if they have a couple of children in graduate school, or perhaps an adult child with a handicap. They were only funded for the owner of the pension and his or her spouse.

Defined-benefit pension plans were difficult to sustain. Companies that offered them gradually sought other options. The expense was considerable. As an employer, you were making a lot of long-term guarantees to a large pool of workers. Each year you would be compelled to put very large pools of money aside. It was fairly common that when a company with a defined-benefit pension plan would run into trouble, it would raid the pension plan. Therefore, large employers were very happy when Congress enacted changes to the IRS code that allowed for tax-exempt retirement savings-and-investment plans—which the employee, not the employer, would in fact be responsible for.

Big corporate employers were happy to tell the workforce what a great new thing these 401(k) plans and IRA accounts would be for them. At first, as so many recall, they were in there with you, shoulder to shoulder, matching all or part of your contribution to your tax-sheltered retirement plan. As we've all seen, that was a temporary transition period, for the most part. The employer match helped establish the 401(k) in peoples' minds as a nice thing, as something that really wasn't such a step down from the 1950s-style pension plan that the employer was responsible for.

In the 25 years since I started my own financial advisory company, the implications of having your retirement savings invested in securities has evolved and changed. Twenty years ago, we were in a bull market. Investors kept seeing their account values go up and up and up. In the '90s there were some mutual funds paying 30 or 40 percent a year. People who were making 20 percent would actually complain about it.

No money was going into the banks for CDs, and less money was going into the insurance companies to buy guaranteed income streams. Investors thought, "My God, the stock market is going great guns. The only way to make money is

Wall Street. It just keeps going up." You would have missed a lot of gains if you weren't on that train, steaming down the track. It was a phenomenon that happened for a number of reasons, but mainly based on demographic causes, driven by the baby boom generation.

If you're part of that generation, you may remember a couple of events that drew attention to difficulties with private corporate pensions. The Kennedy administration was studying the rights of pension beneficiaries, and in the midst of that the Studebaker automobile company closed its plant and went out of business. It turned out that Studebaker's pension plan was so underfunded there was no way it could make good on what it owed to its employees. There was a settlement involving a sliding scale of payments, depending on years of service, but it caused a great outcry. A few years later, the Senate took up legislation to address the funding, vesting, reporting, and disclosure issues identified by the presidential committee.

There was resistance to this idea, from both labor and management, but then a news special on NBC about underfunded pension plans was aired in 1972, and that seemed to be a tipping point. The landmark ERISA bill, standing for Employee Retirement Income Security Act, was passed a couple of years later, in 1974. Then, in 1978, once Congress figured it had fixed the problems in the old corporate-pension system, it passed the Revenue Act of 1978, which included a provision that became

Internal Revenue Code Sec. 401(k). That's the clause in the tax law where the 401(k) plans got their name. The Revenue Act of 1978 added permanent provisions to the tax code, allowing the use of salary reductions as a source of plan contributions. So, the working people of America were given a new law that created a new investment vehicle—but they were also given responsibility, more or less, for saving up for retirement on their own.

Once 401(k)s and IRAs were born, the mutual fund industry got a huge dose of adrenaline. All the employee-deduction dollars for retirement needed somewhere to go, and mutual funds were a fairly obvious choice. Large amounts of money started being fed into 401(k)s and IRAs, and it was all going into Wall Street and caused a boom. "Inflows to mutual funds" was a phrase you heard all the time, and those inflows were constantly increasing, month after month, year after year, and kept running the equities up to the positive side.

We had more people in the workforce. The baby boom generation created a bulge of workers—not to mention the social changes that led to a huge new flow of working women into relatively well-paying jobs. So the system was feeding money, through payroll deductions, into 401(k) plans and into IRAs. The influx drove the market up. That was a root cause of our 20-year bull-market run.

After 2000, when the so-called tech bubble broke, the baby boom generation continued as an important puzzle piece—but since then, there has been a significant difference. We're starting to have more baby boom retirees than boomers in their prime earning years. You no longer have a river of cash flowing one way, into retirement accounts and into the stock market and mutual funds. People are hitting the age when they can take distributions without penalty, which is generally at the age of 59½. They are beginning to pull money out of their IRAs and 401(k)s.

Others, from just ahead of the baby boom group, are at age 70½, when they must take required minimum distributions (RMDs) from their IRA and 401(k) plans. The IRS forces them to take distributions out of the retirement accounts that they were feeding money into over the past 30 years. That money, on the way in, has not been taxed at any point. Now, in retirement, they need that money to start coming out – and that is the IRS's chance to impose a tax on it. The IRS has been waiting, and it wants its share.

So we now have more baby boomer retirees than workers, and it's going to be like this over the next 20 or 30 years. More of them are retiring every day, and more are turning 70½ every day, so now we have a reversal. Instead of all this money going in, all this money's going to be coming out for the retirees' income. There are other factors—for example, the flameout of the banks and brokerages, the mortgage failures. Put it all together, and we are not going to see the market that we saw in the 1980s and '90s. That particular bull market was once in a lifetime.

Most economists are saying that over the next 20 years we're going to have a flat, up-and-down stock market. When the dust settles, it will resemble the flat line we've been looking at for the last 12 years. Flat, with a choppy pattern to it, is what they expect for equity prices.

If you're a retiree, can you afford that gamble? What if you need income and we have a lengthy bear market? Let's say your portfolio is worth $250,000, and it must last the rest of your life, and you're drawing income off of that $250,000. Let's say you're drawing 5 percent a year. Then along comes a bear market, and your $250,000 drops to $175,000. If you want to continue living the same lifestyle, you soon find that 5 percent off $175,000 is not enough. To compensate, you start dipping into your principal—and that's how people run out of money in their retirement years.

The other great contributor to our perception of an IRA or a 401(k) is the tax treatment. In the case of a 401(k), an employee earning an annual salary of $50,000 would have been responsible, under the old rules, for paying income taxes on all of it. However, with the change in the tax laws came an attractive option. Instead of the IRS taking its full 28 percent or 35 percent of that $50,000, the employee would be able to tuck a portion of it, let's say $5,000, into a qualified retirement account. That money would be walled off from the taxman. Rather than taking a portion of the $50,000, the IRS would only get a crack at $45,000.

As most people know, those contributed funds don't escape taxation permanently. They come out of your paycheck and go into the 401(k) without being taxed, and they accrue interest or capital appreciation year to year without being taxed, but in the end the IRS is standing there, waiting for a cut.

If, come retirement, your 401(k) has experienced a lot of growth, that's in part because it has grown "tax-deferred." Your account was channeled into bonds, or mutual funds or stocks, and whatever gains it experienced were also shielded from taxation. Well, Uncle Sam gives and he also takes. The government gave you the advantage of not having to pay tax on a part of your income, nor on the proceeds of putting that money to work, but it wants you to hold up your end of the bargain. So, it will tax your voluntary withdrawals, and eventually compel you to make withdrawals, and tax those. When you finally want the use of your qualified-plan money and begin taking distributions—in a lump sum or through installments—you certainly have to pay the tax on all of it.

Highlights of the Rules on IRA Withdrawals

- All IRA withdrawals are subject to ordinary income tax.

- An additional 10% early distribution penalty tax is assessed if you have not reached at least age 59½ when you take your distribution.

- Before age 59½, you can withdraw from an IRA without suffering the 10 percent penalty if you become disabled, if you are buying a home for the first time, if you have a certain level of medical expenses, or if you are paying certain higher-education expenses.

- You can leave all contributed funds and tax-deferred appreciation in your IRA until April 1 of the calendar year following the year in which you reach 70½. Once that day arrives, you are subject to required minimum distributions, or RMDs. From that point until your death, using a formula based on your life expectancy, you will have to take an RMD every year. If you don't take it, you are subject to a penalty equal to 50 percent of that RMD.

- If you die with IRA funds still in your account, your beneficiary will be paid that balance amount and will have to pay income taxes on it.

Chapter 4

THE VARIABLE ANNUITY: WALL STREET'S FAMOUS LEMON

chapter four

A variable annuity—basically, a Wall Street product with an insurance policy wrapped around it—gives investors a false sense of security. They think they have valuable guarantees, and in some sense they do, but the cost of getting those guarantees is high. Also, it's hard to make money on a variable annuity because of all the charges and the costs. The market must return at least three to five percent every year just for you to break even. Once you're in variable annuities, however, you're stuck. At our firm, we steer clear of them.

Variable annuities are very much like a lot of equity investments you could make, but they use the names of big insurance companies such as Equitable or John Hancock. They therefore have the power of those good names behind them, but they still are a Wall Street product. They come with a prospectus, which means they are a security—and that means two things: There are fees, and you can lose your money. That's why you never get a prospectus with a guaranteed-savings vehicle: There are no fees and risk to principal with a guaranteed-savings account.

Investors can put their money into mutual funds, bonds, or other accounts with no guarantees, or they can put it into a fixed account with a minimum guaranteed interest. Few people opt for that fixed minimum guarantee because it hardly pays anything. If they wanted to allocate their funds into that fixed rate account, they would be better off just buying a fixed annuity without any fees or loads. Their broker who sells it has them in the stock market with the purchase of many different equities. That's how the broker can charge all those fees and loads. They're basically buying mutual funds wrapped inside this annuity.

You could buy the mutual funds a lot cheaper outside the annuity. In the 1990s, when the market was roaring and people were making a lot of money in the market, and they worried about capital gains, the variable annuity was a good tax shelter. Any time you bought and sold, as long as it was inside this annuity, you paid no tax. So that's when variable annuities took off, and it was great when there was a bull market. But when the market started collapsing and savings were wiped out, people realized, "Wait a minute, these are risky, just like being in the market." You're investing in mutual funds and stocks. They go up, they go down. You can lose everything. You might win; you might lose.

Variable annuities are very expensive with fees. Variable annuity fees can run between three and up to five percent per year, and that's whether you make money or lose money. The broker and the insurance company and all the back office is still getting paid every year. To this day hundreds of billions of dollars of these are sold by all the brokerage firms because there's so much profit in them, and a broker makes so much money. They get paid every year that this individual holds that annuity—they get that fee. Let's say the fees total four percent a year; that means, right off the bat, the market has to do at least four just for you to break even. If the market does ten, you're going to net six, after the fees.

A lot of people don't even know these fees are in there because it never shows on the statement, but it's in the contract. This is why people need to read the contract or have it reviewed by a financial professional to be aware of the fees they will have to pay. They actually pay a mortality and expense charge because the variable annuities have a death benefit. If you put in $100,000 and let's say the market drops 50 percent, now your $100,000 is worth $50,000. That death benefit will bring it back up to $100,000, but it costs a fee to have that, and it's very misleading. Also that death benefit is fully taxable.

You are better off buying a life insurance policy for a lot less cost and when you die all proceeds are tax-free. This death benefit gives people a false sense of security. They think, "Oh

I have a death benefit." The difficulty arises if you need your money to live off of, only to find you're living off of $50,000 vs. $100,000. The only way you get that $100,000 is if you die. And of course it will go to your beneficiary. But they will have to pay ordinary income tax on the amount they receive.

What they've done is welded a little life insurance policy onto your annuity. You are the one who pays for it, and that policy is quite expensive. It comes out usually about one and a half percent per year of the total amount of value in that annuity. Now that's just a mortality and expense cost. Then you have the administration charge. Then you still have to pay the cost of those mutual funds, and mutual funds can cost you between one and two percent a year.

Variable annuities also can have a guaranteed income rider attached to them, which is very misleading. It's called a living benefit rider. Let's say that $100,000 is guaranteed to grow at, say, six percent, no matter what happens to the market. So everybody thinks, "Oh great, no matter what happens, I have a six percent guarantee growing in this account." What they don't realize is that the cost of that rider is another one and a half to two percent. So add the 1½ percent there, the two percent in mutual funds cost, and the one and a half percent for the mortality and expense cost.

You're up to five percent right there, and in order to get that guarantee of six percent growth, in most of these you will have to annuitize the contract. Some people jokingly refer to this requirement that you annuitize as "annuicide," because, let's say, in 10 years the market has collapsed and you want to take advantage of that guarantee: You have to sign over all the rights to that cash to the insurance company. You can never cash out with that income value, and they're just going to pay you the rest of that money back as an income for life with little to no interest. It's extremely undesirable as an investment, and really unfair.

The riders or conditions added to contracts often are more important than the terms of the contract itself. The riders are like a smokescreen and help sell the product. The brokers tell the client that no matter what happens in the market, the account is still guaranteed to grow by 6 percent. What they fail to tell the client is that in order to get that guarantee, you have to annuitize the contract, and most people don't know what annuitizing the contract involves—that it means you give up all the rights to that cash.

You give the cash back to the insurance company, and they'll pay you an income stream the rest of your life at a minimal rate of maybe one or even a half percent. Let's say you started with $100,000 and over five years the market drops and it just keeps losing. It goes down to $25,000 but because of that income rider, your $100,000 is worth $150,000. You think, "My God, I can't cash out and get that $150,000. In order to get that guarantee, you have to say, "Okay, I'm annuitizing the contract," and the insurance company takes $150,000 divided by your life expectancy. It will refund the $150,000 to you over your lifetime at a minimal rate of less than 1 percent. Basically, all you're getting is your principal refunded to you over time, with little or no interest. It's a false sense of security.

However, what most people don't realize is that you can't take that income value, the $150,000, and cash it in and walk away with that amount. That $150,000 is paid out over a monthly basis over your lifetime, which will basically come out to literally nothing, not enough to live off of. Let's say you're 65 years old. Let's say you have 20 years of life, so $150,000 divided by 20 comes to $7,500 a year. That's a payment of $625 a month the rest of your life. That is the only way you can get that higher income value on your account. The only cash you have access to is the $50,000 that's the actual value of what the market did to your account.

Wall Street invented variable annuities a number of years ago. Hundreds of billions of dollars a year go into these investment vehicles, thanks to Wall Street's well-known marketing power. The brokers make them sound so good. You get all the upside of the market, they say, and if the markets do fold, don't worry, you have this guarantee at 6 percent. But they bury the details in the fine print. That's not your money if you want it in cash.

Many people then get upset. They want to know, "How do I get out of this thing?" They find out, if they are within the surrender charge period, that getting out means paying a penalty. And yet they don't want to stay in because they might keep losing money, losing principal, through market losses. So it can become a Catch-22.

At the educational workshops I conduct, I tell the audience: "If any of you have a variable annuity, come in, meet with me, I'll review it for you and I'll highlight all the riders I'm talking about in your contract. Bring the contract in and I'll show you how that contract actually works, what the fees are, how much you're paying, and how to get that guarantee." Then we will get on the phone with the insurance company, and I'll have the insurance company representative explain to the client how this guarantee works. Once the client hears it, he or she usually says, "The broker never told me this, or I would have never bought the contract." That happens nine out of ten times.

So they don't know what to do. If they get out of the variable annuity, they're going to get hit with a penalty, but if they stay in, they lose more money. "I can't afford to lose any more money," they tell me. "I'm in my retirement years. This money's supposed to be protected. I told my broker, 'I want to guarantee this principal.'" I have seen this over and over again. The brokers didn't tell them you have to annuitize the contract in order to get the guarantee.

Now if they're lucky and the market was up over the last number of years, they made money. A lot of the people are not that lucky. They suffer a loss, plus they still pay all those annual fees. Variable annuities are one of retirees' biggest complaints.

Chapter 5

WALKING AWAY
FROM WALL STREET
TOWARD GUARANTEED
INSURANCE CONTRACTS

chapter five

Our banking system in the United States, and everywhere else, is backed by the "fractional reserve" system. Banks hold a fraction—a few dollars for every $100 they have out in loans—as their reserve against loans that don't get serviced. By contrast, an insurance company, to comply with its legally chartered reserve requirements, must have one for one. If it has $5 billion in policies underwritten, it has to be sitting on that much in cash reserves, to guarantee that it could pay every dollar back of all the policies' funds in case of severe disruptions, disasters, or whatever negative scenario you want to imagine.

I say cash, but in most cases an insurance company has its reserves parked in bonds. These would be long-term, mid-range or short-term bonds, issued by the Federal Reserve or another extremely stable government entity. I'm talking about solid, investment-grade bonds, not anything resembling a high-yield or "junk" bond. They hold those bonds to maturity. That's how they get full value. When people talk about 30-year Treasury bonds, they are talking about activity in which normal investors are trading in and out of these "long" bonds. Not the insurance companies—they hold 30-year Treasuries for 30 years. No other investor or institution does that.

Insurance companies are different. Their view is extremely long-term. That's why the older ones have been in business, with spotless records of making good on their obligations, for hundreds of years. This book is about retirement security and protected assets that yield a healthy income, so I believe you will find the insurance industry very exciting indeed. It's the key to achieving retirement goals for many people.

Let me pause a moment here to make an important point about the "three stages of money." Each of these stages is connected to a stage of life and also to a certain type of financial institution. I am talking about the phases of your life where bank accounts fit in, where investment accounts fit in, and where insurance accounts fit in.

Stage one is savings, through an account at the local bank. In technical terms they are known as "thrift institutions," and thrift is a nice word that we as a culture should probably try to embrace again. It really ought to be a more important value in our society.

When I was a kid, I wanted a new bike, so I went to my dad and I asked him if I could get one. He said, "Sure you can." I was elated. I stood there thinking: Wow—I'm getting a new bike. So I said, "Can we go to the store right now?" My father answered: "We could, but don't you think you need some money?" I assumed he was going to pay for it, but I was wrong.

He told me I could get this new bicycle once I had earned and saved enough money to pay for it. To do that, I started mowing lawns. I shoveled driveways. I did odd jobs and started saving my money. When I had a little bit of cash piled up, I needed a place to put it, so I went with my father down to the local bank. I opened up my first savings account. I wanted my money to be safe and liquid. The first financial institution we are all introduced to is a bank. We need banks for emergencies. You should have at least three to six months of regular expenses in savings at a bank. The rate of return should not matter. Return is almost irrelevant. Odds are good that you will have some sort of money in the bank the rest of your life. Even if you die at 95, you will still have some money in the bank.

What happens next, after the savings stage? We get older. Some of us go off to college. We get our first real job or start our careers. We start earning a real income. We are reaching adulthood, and that's when we reach stage-two, investments. It's time to accumulate money so at some point we can be financially secure and independent. We move through life transitions, and with that movement comes money transitions.

We move from safe and liquid to a stage that involves risk and return. We focus on different investment options. We're trying to build a portfolio, and thus we are looking for rate of return. The purpose of stage two is accumulation and growth. Think about how you pick your mutual funds and your 401(k) investments. You tend to look for a long track record of positive returns, even though Wall Street will always state that past performance does not guarantee future results. We accept that, but we look past it, because we hope the good years, when we're experiencing growth, outweigh the bad years, when we're suffering losses. Our purpose is to grow and accumulate money until we reach retirement. This is the stage of the brokerage houses in Wall Street. We turn for investment service to companies with names like Merrill Lynch, Smith Barney, Morgan Stanley, UBS, Schwab, Fidelity, Vanguard, and Edward Jones. Even if we live to the age of 95, we will still have some money in these types of accounts.

However, once we reach the age of retirement and/or financial independence, we need to shift to stage three. That's the stage of preservation and income. We're taking our portfolio and transitioning from growth and accumulation. This is the stage where we are enjoying the fruits of our labor. At this point, we want to generate safe and sustainable lifetime income. We want to enjoy lifetime income that is contractually guaranteed.

In stage three, lifetime income becomes a very important part of your world view. This is your retirement lifestyle. Your lifestyle in retirement depends on the amount of guaranteed income you have coming in for the rest of your life. This is the point at which we're using accounts like guaranteed insurance contracts (GICs), annuities, and income riders. The source of these important tools is the insurance industry. Basically we are talking about the life insurance companies that specialize in living and death benefits.

Because life insurance companies operate their core business around compensation for death, and their policies have to be paid in every legitimate case, they are closely regulated. Likewise, their requirements for funds in reserve could not be more stringent. For that reason, they are the only entity in the financial world that could reasonably be expected to reliably sell and service guaranteed insurance contracts.

Few people know that this type of investment has been around for over a hundred years. During the 1930s, banks failed at an alarming rate, and it was the insurance industry that bailed out the banks when so many of them collapsed. Because of that, insurance companies get preferential tax treatment. It's something they earned based on their historic strength. It is also why insurance companies can pay more return than a bank. Insurance companies on their internal profit pay no tax, whereas banks have to pay it. Plus, not only does the insurance company get preferential tax treatment, you as the owner of a guaranteed insurance contract otherwise known as an annuity, get excellent tax treatment, too. When you put your money in, it grows tax-deferred. The policyholder pays no tax as it grows. That's the case even though the investment vehicle is not within an IRA, which is one of the biggest advantages of a guaranteed insurance contract with an insurance company. Without setting up an additional IRA, you get the advantages of an IRA. You pay no tax on yearly growth. Only when you pull money out will you get a Form 1099 mailed to you. But during the term of the contract you don't receive any 1099 forms because all the growth is tax-deferred.

This whole process is not new. It has unfolded like this for many years. Remember the old pension plans? They were accounts, issued only by insurance companies that would guarantee income for life. Corporate pensions were a sweet spot in the history of retirement income planning. However, we got off track. This occurred because, in the 1980s and 1990s, stage two took on a new look. The stock market had a long positive bull cycle. Things on Wall Street went really, really well. What happened was all the people who were retiring then were starting to shift a lot of their funds to the insurance companies—buying guaranteed income contracts, such as guaranteed annuities.

Wall Street looked their way and said, "Whoa, hold on there. What are you doing?"

They made a pitch to the American worker who was trying to transition from stage two to stage three. Brokerage people got on the phone and said: "Look at how well you've been doing. Look at how much money you've been making in your accounts. You're making 20 percent or more a year. Why would you want to move it over there and make less return? We are smarter now. We can create asset allocation models. You should just keep your money here in stage two."

Wall Street, which has tight ties to the financial publications, started putting out that message, and it was very well-received. The question you may still have is: What's wrong with that? What's wrong with staying in stage two for retirement income planning? The prospect of bear markets is primarily what's wrong with that plan. We all learned that from 2000 to 2002, when we had a major market crash, and then we learned it again in 2008 through 2009.

Are markets always performing well? Of course not. When markets are not doing so well, everything goes to pot. Most of you are familiar with how the brokerage industry says to build a balanced portfolio in stage two and withdraw 4 percent a year. If you do that, there's a 75 percent chance you will never run out of money. Let me ask you about 75 percent chances:

That isn't good enough to get you on a plane, is it? Imagine if you were buckled in for your flight and the pilot came on and said, "We have clear skies and there's a 75 percent chance we will arrive safely, but there's a 25 percent chance we're going to crash and burn." I don't know about you, but I'd be getting off the plane and driving instead. Wall Street and the brokerage industry think that's good-enough odds for retirees for the rest of their lives. My argument is: No, it's not. The people we serve deserve better.

They deserve to have a comfortable retirement regardless of which way the markets are moving, and the only way you can do that is to make sure you transition sufficient assets into stage three accounts. By sufficient, we mean enough assets so that you can contractually guarantee your lifetime income. That means you will be getting a check every single month for the rest of your life regardless of what the markets do. Does that mean we should move every single dollar out of stage one and stage two? Of course we don't do that. We need to transfer a portion into stage three accounts.

How much should we transition? Putnam—which is a stage-two mutual fund company, mind you—did a study in July 2011. The report said a retiree should have no more than 25 percent in stage two, or money at risk. So that means if you have a million dollars, Putnam says $250,000 is the most you should have at risk in stage two. All the other money should be transferred over to stage three. That's preservation and income, not growth and risk.

In my own practice, the 75-25 might be a good fit for some clients, but I do remind them that if they consider that to be too conservative, they should consult the classic Rule of 100 guideline. As you recall, you subtract your age from 100 and allow the result to be your percentage of assets left in the growth-and-risk category, i.e., stage two. If you're 65 years old, that means 35 percent is the most you should have at risk and 65 percent should be guaranteed and preserved. The Rule of 100 has been around for years, and now you have Putnam saying that's not enough safety, that 25 percent is the most you should have at risk. One must set one's own ratio, based on sound advice.

"I can't afford to risk anything," some of my clients say. "I want it all safe. I want it all preserved." That attitude results partly from fatigue and regret at losses they have incurred. It's not uncommon to hear the statement, "I'm tired of taking risks. I'm tired of seeing my retirement account dwindle." People who say this realize that when they stop working, there's no way they can build that retirement account back up. The money isn't coming in.

So, when you come to an advisory firm like mine and decide to put money in a guaranteed annuity, you are putting up a sum of money that will come back to you at some point in the future with fixed, scheduled payments and upside growth potential to help it continually grow. It gives you fully protected principal and the opportunity for gains beyond the interest income. The insurance company makes money by earning a slightly higher interest rate on the bond it purchases than the rate it contracted to pay you. It doesn't impose a management fee or maintenance fee, so the cost to own this investment is extremely minimal. Meanwhile—and this will be explained—there are now significant upside growth and appreciation possibilities with these investments.

You probably never told yourself that money-management and retirement security would be something you could accomplish by turning from the securities industry—Wall Street, for short—to the insurance industry. You may never have had that thought consciously, but it's the right one, and it's what I strongly suggest you do.

Chapter 6

SAFETY MEETS GROWTH IN A FIXED INDEX ANNUITY

chapter six

The newest breed of guaranteed insurance contracts are index-linked. It came out in the mid-1990s during a bull market, with portfolios increasing in value dramatically. People were making 30 to 40 percent on mutual funds in a year. Banks and insurance companies were trying to sell their CDs and their fixed annuities, at low interest rates— and they were being ignored by people who had investable savings. So one of the commercial banks, I think it was Chase Manhattan, came out with an index-linked CD. It said, "We can sell you a CD, but we'll tie the returns to a stock index." That was the beginning of the index-linked CD, which gave rise to the index-linked annuity.

The insurance companies almost always service the safety-oriented investor better than banks can, so they went to the drawing board. They came to the conclusion that they could use their cash-rich position and more controlled risk scenarios to offer a similar product to the market-linked CD, only with a better rate and better terms. The thinking of the insurance executives was along the lines of: "We can do this better than the banks because we have more cash. We don't loan our money out. We have an immense bond portfolio. We have a higher rate of return and profit. Our reserves and surplus are not subject to tax. We can do an index-linked contract that really pays off for the investor."

Investing in one of these contracts is a wise step toward safety, with a fine possibility of measurable growth. First off, it means your principal is guaranteed. You can never lose it. It pays you a minimum rate of return, but your earnings are tied to a stock index, usually the Standard & Poor's 500 index. Your money is not directly in the market, so you have none of the risk.

What the insurance companies designed was a hybrid product. They came up with a means by which your money is guaranteed, but with higher growth potential than a CD based on the growth of a stock index. You can't lose your principal or previous gains with this type of account. You have a minimum lifetime guarantee no matter what the market does. In addition, you get the upside growth potential because the returns are tied in part, to the upside of a stock index.

On these index-linked accounts, you can take a fixed rate or you can opt for the link to an equity market index, or you can do both. That's the "hybrid" part. In every way you gain more flexibility. At the start of each year, you have the right to decide between allocating your account to a fixed rate or tying it to the S&P 500 index. If you choose the latter, your worst-case scenario in a down market is pretty benign—your account doesn't lose money, it doesn't get clipped by fees, but on your investment for that year you get a zero return since there was no growth in the index for that year.

Once the investing public began to understand how these hybrid accounts worked, they responded enthusiastically, and over time this product has steadily grown in popularity. In 1997 about $3 billion was invested this way. By 2008, about $26 billion was invested in these accounts, and in 2010, over $30 billion went into them. Every year they're getting more and more popular because there are more and more people who want a higher return than what CDs offer, but they don't want to dive into the stock market and risk losses. This product fits right in between CDs and the stock market in terms of risk and reward.

Security comes from knowing you have a guaranteed contract with an insurance company. The insurance company has to provide the guarantees because it's all backed by legal reserves and its cash surplus. The company guarantees that the principal you put up will always be there. It guarantees it will grow at a minimum rate regardless of what the market does, yet it does have a way to give you the potential for higher returns.

In managing these accounts, the insurance company is not trying to outguess, outthink, or outperform the market. It basically places enough money in U.S. Treasury bonds, at a guaranteed rate of return, to be assured it can cover the minimum guaranteed payout to you. Once it has done that, it takes whatever sum is left over and uses a portion of it on Wall Street to purchase an option on the S&P 500 index. To understand the wisdom in the design of these contracts, you have to understand how stock options work—but you don't have to know all the intricacies of the entire options market. You only have to understand what a "call" option is and how the insurance companies use them, which is not all that complicated.

An option gives you the right to buy, but you are not obligated to buy. That's why it's called an option. If the S&P 500 is up for the year, the insurance company exercises its right on the option and captures a portion of the gain. However if the S&P 500 is down, it is not obligated to buy, so that option expires, worthless. So in that year there is no gain, but your principal and previous gains are protected from market loss. Zero is the worst your account can fare in a down market, yet you can be proud of that zero, considering you have not lost and cannot lose your money.

There is no risk, therefore, to the insurance company or to the client. Yes, they watch the stock market all year and root for it to go up, but they aren't like the people who actually buy stocks and mutual funds. Those people have ownership in the stock market and therefore are risking their hard-earned principal. When you own equities, you own the ups and you also own the downs. You own the losses.

You might think you could enjoy this risk-reward benefit as an investor by buying options yourself. As you might expect, the advantage in working with an insurance company is its ability to buy options a lot cheaper than you and I could, given the billions of dollars it invests. Also, it is using yield to buy that option, whereas the typical investor would be using principal.

Instead of buy-and-hold, the path to success in the stock market is to buy low, sell high. The problem is, you need a crystal ball to do that with consistent success. This form of investing puts buy and sell on autopilot. It buys low. It locks in the gain automatically for you on the anniversary date of your account. You get the growth without risking your life savings. These financial products do have caps on the upside growth potential, which will be explained in more detail later, and that's where the cost of the option comes in. But you never have a negative year and only get the upside of the stock index. Your return ends up a lot higher than other safe investments such as CDs.

In a down year, you have faced an opportunity cost but you have endured no actual loss of wealth.

Where the investor in equities goes wrong, obviously, is taking a large percentage loss on a significant portion of his wealth—and then making a comeback of sorts, followed by another large percentage loss. We might be talking about an investor who in 2005 does beautifully—we'll say he made seven percent that year. With that success, of course, he stays in the market. In 2007 he is up another five or six percent. But along comes 2008 and his wealth goes down 40 to 50 percent.

It's up, down, up, down. A long, long time goes by, and that person's wealth has not grown at all. From 1999 to 2011, the stock market had a net gain of nothing. It's very tough to recover from all those lost years. And don't forget that the investor is still paying all those fees and loads to the brokerage houses and Wall Street, even while losing significant amounts of money.

By contrast, when I talk with my investors, we use the phrase "the power of zero." Riding the ups and downs of Wall Street for a decade and netting zero is a dismal result that is going to affect your long-term quality of life. However, in these index accounts, a zero generally means that the index went down for that period. It also means you've had zero losses. Your wealth has lived to fight another day and that day is coming right up, with the law of averages favoring you.

"Zero becomes your hero" is another phrase we use. If you get a zero percent return, that means all the people in equities lost money. You didn't lose a dime. You just didn't get a rate of return for that year. That's when zero becomes powerful to you.

My clients who own these hybrid accounts don't walk around anxiously. They don't worry when they turn on the cable-TV financial channels or open up the morning newspaper to the stock pages. During that period when the market was down, they shrugged their shoulders when they looked at the news, and at night they slept like a baby. They have peace of mind. They have a worry-free retirement, and that's why people buy these products. They don't want to wake up every morning worried about how the market is doing. As in: "Oh my god, I'm down another 200 or 300 points, which means I'm losing $30,000 today!" That's stress. In retirement, that's not what you want. Instead, you can take comfort in the minimum yield guarantee, irrespective of stock market performance.

And here's another important advantage to the hybrid account: You can take distributions. You can receive an income for life, and you can make withdrawals every year up to 10 percent without any penalty or charge. This is a free with-drawal—no charge associated with it whatsoever, no fees, no penalty. These accounts are more flexible and liquid than CDs are.

Bear in mind, you obviously are lowering your principal when you withdraw funds, but that is your money and your choice. What really matters is you have access to money in case of a sudden need. I have many clients who open up these accounts for 10 years or another length of time, while asking for the annual interest to be paid out monthly. With the balance in their accounts, they still get the market's upside.

An example would be the client who entered into one of these contracts on, let's say, June 1, 2011. The insurance company and the client take note of what the S&P 500 index is on that date. A year later on June 1, 2012, they look at the index's closing. And if the market went up eight percent, the client will get a good portion of that gain.

The insurance company can offer you a very good investment product, with peace of mind and a chance for significant gains. I can assure you that my clients are happy they made the investment. I have hundreds of clients who own this product, and I am proud to say that none has ever experienced a loss of any kind. Indeed, they have been earning more than what CDs pay.

Skeptical clients sometimes wonder why an investment like the one I'm describing isn't widely known. People figure that if a superior product comes to market and is available for a period of years, with highly satisfied customers, they should know all about it already. These contracts are indeed growing in popularity at a steady clip, and the general awareness of them is rising. However, the insurance industry's traditional ideas about marketing come into play.

When a product comes along offering distinct advantages and solving all sorts of problems, Americans expect it's going to be advertised and promoted. But insurance, particularly life insurance, is a carefully considered purchase that people try not to dwell upon, since it involves the rather unpleasant subject of untimely death. There's a saying in the industry "No one has ever bought a life insurance policy. If they own one, it's because somebody sold it to them." No matter how relieved or glad a person is after purchasing life insurance, they still might have gone years without doing so if an agent hadn't sat down with them to directly explain its importance.

Therefore, advertising and marketing don't come that easily to those in the insurance industry—it's not their strong suit. Some of these companies have been around for centuries, so their traditions are all that much deeper and more abiding. In general, the same traditions and customs that help make insurance companies financially strong keep them from jumping into the modern ways of marketing.

Meanwhile, Wall Street has put out many negative articles about these products, without studying or fully understanding them. Most of the brokerage firms on Wall Street do not offer these types of accounts. They do not make a dime from these products—they are not securities, after all; they are guaranteed insurance contracts. Wall Street would rather have your money in equities under management and collect all those fees from you every year. So the only way you would hear about this type of investment account would be from an independent advisor who educated you on it or if someone referred you to an advisor who offers this type of savings vehicle.

If this all sounds attractive as an investment, it will sound better as we discuss the upgrades and improvements that have been made to these index annuities in recent years. There is a newer breed of these hybrid accounts. They've become more sophisticated in their design. Now instead of having caps on the upside potential of these accounts, you can now own one of these accounts without any "caps" or limits placed on the upside earnings potential of the S&P 500 index. Ultimately, this provides you with the opportunity to realize above-average long-term accumulation compared to other common financial products (i.e. savings accounts, bank CDs, etc.) particularly in times of low interest rates.

All this, plus you get the peace of mind that comes from knowing your account is protected from any losses due to market fluctuation. For the investor, they aren't more complicated—except that you have some more options and benefits to consider. But in their internal operation, they are very refined and improved.

There are three worlds of money you can invest in. In the world of safety and guarantees, there are CDs you can buy, there are government bonds and Treasury notes, and there are fixed annuities. They are all safe money instruments and are all guaranteed from any stock market risk, but the problem is they lack growth potential.

In the world of risk and Wall Street, you can invest in mutual funds, stocks, bonds, ETFs, variable annuities, and REITS, but they have no guarantees and you can lose your money. They do have growth potential, though, and that is the trade-off.

Then in the mid 1990s, a new world of investments came onto the scene: the hybrid accounts. They are Fixed Index Annuities, and they fit right in between the banks and Wall Street. They are the best of both worlds. They give you safety and guarantees, but they also give you upside growth potential. That gives you the ability to earn above-average returns without risking your principal or previous gains.

In the three worlds of money, they fit right in the middle.

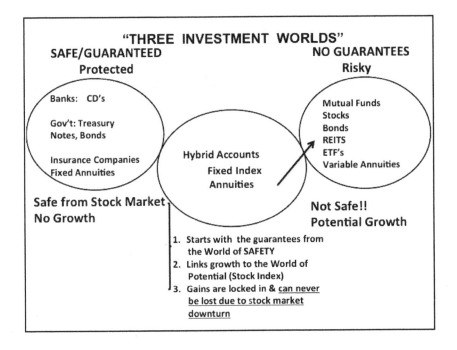

If you would like more information on how this account works, contact me at 314-993-9494.

Chapter 7

TURNING RETIREMENT SAVINGS INTO A PERSONAL PENSION

chapter seven

My financial advisory practice is all about retirement, so my focus is constantly on income. By that I mean guaranteed, regular, reliable, adequate income for the life of the retired individual or couple.

It is immensely satisfying to help make that goal come true for a client, but it's a big challenge. The people who come to me have worked, they have saved, they've done some investing—for better or worse—and they have assets. Now they are sitting across a table from me, and we are answering this question: How do we guarantee them sufficient income for as long as they need it?

If you're reading this book, you very likely have some savings and you have it with a custodian. That custodian, as noted previously, is either a bank, Wall Street, or the insurance industry. One of those three institutions is where you will find all the personal cash savings in the U.S. economy, unless it's in a wall safe or under your mattress.

At some point, in your retirement years, you might need to turn that savings into income. Many, if not most, people go about doing that. Wherever you've placed your savings, if that sum of money is not guaranteed, your income is not guaranteed. You can't have a guaranteed income from a non-guaranteed account.

Sounds obvious, but it's a fact that is lost on many people. Safe money, and income streaming safely from it, is only found in a few places. Most common are CDs and Treasury bonds. They're both safe, and they both guarantee interest income. The problem with each of these two options is yield: The interest rates are too low, especially in the post-2008 financial environment.

So, taking you from the limited world of CDs and Treasuries to something considerably more flexible and beneficial, let's take a look now at the fixed index annuity with guaranteed income riders. A rider is a condition on a contract. It is an option you could add to your contract—one that addresses the retirement income question in a very effective way.

Here's how guaranteed lifetime income riders work. Let's say a man or woman, at age 65, places $200,000 into one of these accounts and decides to add this lifetime income rider to it. Doing so will generate about $10,600 minimum annual income, for life.

That income is guaranteed for life, but you still keep control of your remaining principal, which means you're generating an income for life, and upon death, whatever balance of that principal amount remains will go to your heirs. That's if you continued the payouts through to your time of death. Conversely, if you decide to stop the income stream, you could walk away with whatever remaining principal you have in that account.

If what I've just stated causes you to think back to our discussion of annuitization, your instincts are correct. These income riders are the remedy for the big problems associated with annuitization. "Income for life" always sounds good, but so often it will require the holder of a contract to take that irrevocable step and annuitize their contract.

The income rider on your index annuity account provides what can best be described as a personal pension for you and your spouse. This feature will guarantee, no matter the performance of the underlying index, that your money will grow at a specified rate anywhere between four and eight percent annually up to the point you start your income stream. The value of this account may then be used to determine the amount of lifetime income you will receive and/or be guaranteed at a future date. What makes this lifetime income rider appealing is that once the income stream is started or begun, that income is guaranteed for life regardless of the performance of the underlying stock index—because as you will recall, these are linked to an index.

While index annuities typically have no out-of-pocket operating charges, with this feature you pay a fee, but it's very small—especially so when the benefits are all tallied. The rider will carry a fee for the lifetime income benefit that is usually between a half percent and 0.95 percent. The fee comes out of the account value that you leave your family at death. In other words, at some point in the future if you pass away, there may still be funds remaining in the annuity that could be passed on as a lump sum to your beneficiaries.

This investment guarantees you can withdraw a certain percentage out of your account for the rest of your life. And whatever percentage you start at, it will never decrease. Even though you're taking it for life, that income never decreases, and you take it as long as you live. That would be the case even if there were zero growth in the equities market the entire time you drew income. At some point, if you were in another type of equities investment, you could run out of money. If you keep withdrawing five or six percent income out of your account and you're not getting growth, you're going to run out of money.

That cannot happen with this type of account even if your account value runs down to zero. The annual payout amount you specified originally is guaranteed for life, and the income never stops.

That's why I referred to it as a personal pension. It greatly resembles the old defined-benefit employer pensions. Some people who set themselves up in this vehicle are going to derive more money in income than they put in, because they will have outlived their expected age of mortality, according to the actuarial tables.

Let's say you put $100,000 into the index-linked account. Let's say the market goes up and down over the next decade—up some years, flat some years, down in some years. But on a cumulative basis it is up over the 10-year life of this account. When the dust settles, the $100,000 you deposited has grown to $150,000.

Meanwhile, you have your guaranteed lifetime income value, which is that lifetime benefit option. Let's say that's growing at a guarantee of seven percent. You put in 100,000, kept it there for 10 years, earned seven percent each year, and after 10 years that statement says $200,000. You haven't been touching it, but your situation changes so you go to the insurance company to withdraw income. Here is what is explained to you: You will be drawing your income off of that $200,000. But if you pass away or walk away with cash, you or your beneficiary will receive the $150,000; that's your actual value.

Think of it this way: We buy insurance on our home to protect our home, car insurance to protect our cars from loss, and life insurance to protect against loss of life or health. So, why not buy insurance on your income? What you're doing is you're guaranteeing your value is going to grow at a certain amount of interest every year, regardless of what the market does, and down the road you could turn on an income stream that is guaranteed for life. You're insuring your lifetime income. This guarantees you can never run out of money, which is the biggest concern to most retirees.

If you make a subsequent decision to turn off the income stream, you can do that. You can turn the income off. That's the beauty of these guaranteed contracts with lifetime income riders. You're not annuitizing. So you can start and stop your income at any time. You can turn it on, and then if you don't need the money down the road, you can make a phone call and turn it off so that your account value keeps growing.

These income riders are immensely popular. Almost everybody now getting started with this style of account wants to include the lifetime income rider. I give people the option to take the rider, and they shrug as they consider the advantages: "Why wouldn't I want this guarantee?" they say. "I'm getting a guaranteed growth rate of seven percent for the next 10 or 20 years regardless of what the market does. I can go to sleep at night knowing I have a guaranteed compounding rate of seven percent every year. And when I decide to start income, I'm going to have that value to just draw income from." So imagine that the market did nothing over the next 15 years. You have that compounded growth of, let's say, 7 percent, so you're going to have a lot of money generating you an income for life. You're guaranteeing it, so you'll never run out of money. If you keep your retirement savings on Wall Street, there is never a guarantee you will have any growth, nor can you guarantee an income from those accounts.

Depending on the company and the product you have, there will be a minimum investment. People move from CDs and other types of accounts into these index accounts when their assets have reached a certain level and they're more serious about their investment goals.

There are hundreds of insurance companies and many of these index annuities. It's my job as an independent advisor to filter through all of them and find the best contract and return for right now. "Who has the highest payout?" is one of several questions. There are many different index contracts, and I have no allegiance to any insurance company. My allegiance is to the client. My task is to show the client which company has the best terms and growth potential and the best payout at any given time.

Chapter 8

HOW TO TURN YOUR IRA INTO A "FAMILY LEGACY"

chapter eight

n this chapter, I will discuss effective ways for you to get the most out of your qualified retirement plans. By qualified retirement plans, we mean IRAs, 401(k)s, 403Bs, TSAs, and SEPs. As you may know, those initials stand for: Individual Retirement Account, Tax-Sheltered Annuity, and Self-Employed Pension.

With so many of my clients, the finishing touch on the qualified-plan work we do together is to turn the IRA into a "Family Legacy IRA." In 1974, Congress passed the Employee Retirement Income Security Act, a.k.a., ERISA. That law gave birth to the IRA and the 401(k) plan. The purpose of those accounts was to give Americans more incentive to plan for their retirement and become less dependent on Uncle Sam.

Are there any catches to these retirement accounts? Yes there are. I call them "tax prisons" because there's a 10 percent penalty for early withdrawals if you pull any money out of these retirement accounts before the age of 59½. And there's a 50 percent penalty if you fail to take your required minimum distributions (RMDs) starting at age 70½. And all distributions are fully taxable.

Your IRA can quickly turn into an "Internal Revenue Account." Owners of IRAs and 401(k)s can lose between 40 percent and 80 percent of their IRAs to taxes. That means your IRA quickly becomes an IOU to the IRS. If you are married and pass away, your IRA can transfer tax free to your spouse—however, after the death of both spouses, all funds in that IRA are fully taxable to your heirs.

Here's the good news. The rules have changed. Under the old rules, there were eight methods for calculating distributions, and if you picked the wrong method, it triggered a faster distribution, which meant higher taxes.

The new IRA tax laws benefit the whole family, even the extended family. Under the old rules, children and grandchildren of a deceased IRA account owner had to pay all taxes on their inherited IRA within five years. Under the new rules, they can spread the taxes over their lifetime, which means a $350,000 IRA can pay out more than $1.3 million over three generations just by taking advantage of the new tax laws and allowing untapped principal to grow. (I'm assuming a 4 percent rate of return in my illustration). Let's take the example of Mr. and Mrs. Jones, residents of Missouri.

Example: The Jones
IRA Balance $350,000

Mr. Jones	age	62
Mrs. Jones	age	60
Child 1	age	23
Child 2	age	20
Grandchild	age	4
Grandchild	age	3

Mr. Jones is age 62. Mrs. Jones is age 60. They have two children, ages 23 and 20. They also have two grandchildren, ages 4 and 3. Mr. Jones has an IRA balance of $350,000, and at age 70½ he has to start taking his required minimum distributions and he has to take that out through his life expectancy. If he lives through his life expectancy, which is about the age of 83, he will have pulled out $329,228. Upon death, he leaves a balance to Mrs. Jones in the amount of $458,232 because that IRA account balance has grown again, assuming a 4 percent rate of return.

Mrs. Jones has to begin taking required minimum distributions over her remaining life expectancy, and she'll pull out an additional $81,930. Upon her death, the balance left to the heirs is $416,341. Child number one inherits 30 percent; that's $124,902. Under the old rules if this child takes this out in a lump sum, all taxes are due. He's going to lose approximately 41 percent. Where do we get that percentage? It's 35 percent for the federal income tax and 6 percent for the state of Missouri income tax. As you can see, that $124,902 takes a beating under the old tax rules.

When I walk my clients through this example of the Jones, I stop and ask: Do you think tax rates are going up or down in the future—given all this government spending? Of course taxes are going to go up so by the time their children inherent from them. The rates could be 50 percent or more. But if this child takes the required minimum distribution over his or her own life expectancy, it will pay this child out $228,034 in lifetime income. That's just for child number one.

Child number two inherits the same 30 percent. Once again, the sum is $124,902. If that second child takes it all at once, she loses about half, but if she takes it out over her life expectancy, it will pay her about $239,637.

Now remember, the Joneses have two grandchildren. The first grandchild inherits 20 percent, which is $83,268. If that grandchild pulls the whole sum out at once, he loses over half of it. If he takes it out over his lifetime, it will pay out $212,151. In the case of the younger grandchild, the inherited sum is again 20 percent, or $83,268. By stretching distributions over her full life expectancy, the second grandchild will receive over $216,185. So add all of the RMDs up, and total IRA distributions paid out over three generations comes to $1,307,164. That's just by taking advantage of the new tax laws.

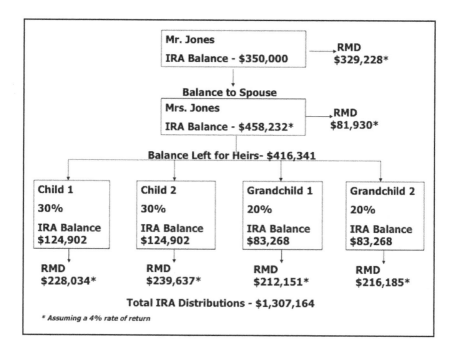

In my workshops, I ask how many people have never heard of this new tax law.

Most people raise their hands and say, "I've never heard of this." And I ask why their brokers or advisors have not educated them on this. This tax law came out in 2002. Stretching out those distributions makes a big difference, but still most people have never heard of this. I also ask the workshop audience: "Do you think your children or grandchildren know about these tax laws?" Of course they don't, so if the kids don't know about this tax law they don't ever take advantage of it. It never gets done, and that's a problem.

We educate our clients. We show them how to turn their retirement accounts into the "Family Legacy IRA." We show them how to set this up automatically without any cost, so when they die they're not going to leave a tax burden to the kids. Instead they are going to leave an income for life.

On a regular $350,000 IRA without the stretch, the payout would be $787,460. With the stretch, it will pay out $1,307,164. That's how the IRA becomes a family legacy, keeping your money all in the family.

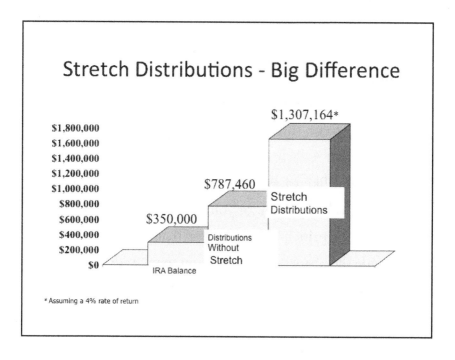

I will explain the effect of all this for one of the grandchildren, whom we'll call Annie. When Mr. and Mrs. Jones have passed away and the grandchild Annie has her inheritance via a stretch or Family Legacy IRA, her required minimum distribution on that $83,268 was only $1,533.

The nice thing about this is that she is going to get this every year for the rest of her life. We can set it up so that these beneficiaries, the children or grandchildren, will get this check every year for the rest of their lives on their birthdays. On the check, at the bottom, would be the words "Happy Birthday from Mom and Dad" or "from Grandma and Grandpa." It's a birthday present every year for the rest of their lives, and the insurance companies are the only custodians who will do this free of charge because they've been doing it for years. Insurance companies have been in the business for 200 years of making lifetime distributions and lifetime payments. So they're set up automatically to do this.

I would like to ask you: Are your IRA funds in a safe place? The ideal custodian for your IRA should do three things: guarantee your principal, administer that IRA free of charge, and provide the proper documentation to take advantage of this new tax law. Let me also ask: Is Wall Street a good custodian for your IRA? Perhaps not. Wall Street exposes your principal to risk; Wall Street charges fees and loads; and Wall Street has the worst documentation on distributing that IRA according to the tax laws. It assumes no responsibility on the distributions of that IRA after the owner's death.

If you had your IRA in a fixed index annuity, you would face no fees or loads. So if you had $416,341 in your IRA in one of those accounts and you had to take out four percent a year of required minimum distributions, how much does your account have to earn if you don't want to spend down that principal? The answer is simple: four percent. If you're drawing out four, you have to at least make four to not touch your principal. And don't forget Wall Street would be busy charging between one and three percent in fees and loads. It's an average of two percent per year. That means on a Wall Street IRA, you have to make at least six percent per year just to break even. And that's assuming you never have a down market. That's a huge difference.

In the year following Mrs. Jones' death, as we showed, the granddaughter Annie had to draw off $1,533. Meanwhile, the broker and his firm that handled the IRA account got about $8,326 in fees. Where do we get that figure? We take $416,341 times two percent as the load or fee. That's $8,326 per year that Wall Street takes out of this IRA account. So I ask you, who becomes the primary beneficiary of your IRA? Is it your heirs, or is it Wall Street?

It's Wall Street. The broker is getting over $8,000 a year in fees. Wall Street is getting more every year than your kids or your grandkids are getting. That's the high cost of small fees if you leave your IRA on Wall Street.

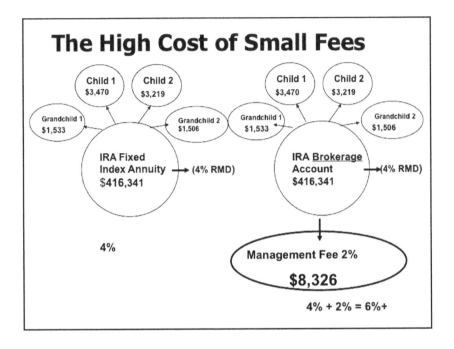

So without using the new tax laws and creating the Family Legacy IRA, that means the account only paid out $827,499, vs. over $1.3 million. Mr. Jones' $350,000 IRA, in our example, paid out over $1.3 million because it was in a fixed index annuity with no fees.

How would you like to take your distributions from your IRA and be guaranteed to leave more money to your spouse or beneficiaries regardless of market fluctuation? This is one of the things we show our clients how to do. But you can only do that with a certain fixed index annuity.

The IRS has two important rules to help you take advantage of the new tax laws. There's a "designated beneficiary" rule and a "separate account" rule. The designated beneficiary rule means that to be eligible to take a lifetime income rather than a fully taxable lump sum distribution from an inherited IRA, you must set up designated beneficiaries. Here's what the separate account rule means: Each beneficiary share must be divided into separate accounts. If separate accounts are not established, the life expectancy of the oldest beneficiary will apply to all beneficiaries. You can learn more in IRS Publication 590, which is the IRA bible for the IRS. It contains all the rules covering IRAs.

This should be done before the death of the account owner. You want to set this up properly, to the letter. IRA owners have two options to set up beneficiaries. You can use a pass-through trust or you can use a restricted beneficiary form. If you're using a trust for your IRA, the beneficiaries cannot use the separate account rule, as Publication 590 specifies. As a result, the IRA funds in the pass-through trust will be paid out under the shortest life expectancy in the pool of heirs, versus everybody getting to stretch it out further.

There is a special IRA Inheritance Trust you can set up if you can find the few attorneys who are familiar with all the tax laws regarding passing IRA accounts to children and grandchildren. We are very proud to work with a knowlegable attorney locally who is an expert at doing this.

You very much want to learn what the restricted beneficiary form does. It lets you decide who inherits your IRA. It lets you decide how the money is to be paid to your beneficiaries. It complies with the designated beneficiary rule, and it complies with the separate account rule, and it guarantees that all required minimum distributions will be paid out to the owner, the spouse, the children and grandchildren, every year for the rest of their lives, and it will avoid that 50 percent tax penalty.

This form is free and sets everything up. It doesn't cost a dime. Only the insurance industry has this form. The brokerage industry and the banks do not have it. In order to qualify for these new tax laws, you have to roll all your company sponsored plans into an IRA. Thus, if you have a 401(k) or an SEP or a TSA, 403B, all those have to be rolled into an IRA in order for you to qualify for this tax law to stretch it out.

In working with clients, my next step in the family legacy process is to ask if they have set up a formal distribution plan. I ask if they have set up the proper designated beneficiaries. Finally, I will ask if they have designated and set up the separate accounts.

It's a multistep process, but it's absolutely worth the effort for anyone with a long-range vision for wealth and family security.

Retirement
Advisory
Group

To learn more about safe retirement
strategies, please call **Thomas Helbig** at
314-993-9494, or email him at
thomas@retirementkey.com.

Visit **www.retirementkey.com** for
information on seminars,
workshops and services.

Notes

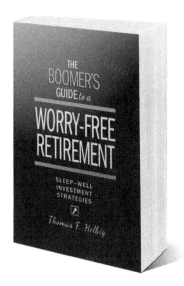

How can you use this book?

MOTIVATE

EDUCATE

THANK

INSPIRE

PROMOTE

CONNECT

Why have a custom version of *The Boomer's Guide to a Worry Free Retirement?*

- Build personal bonds with customers, prospects, employees, donors, and key constituencies

- Develop a long-lasting reminder of your event, milestone, or celebration

- Provide a keepsake that inspires change in behavior and change in lives

- Deliver the ultimate "thank you" gift that remains on coffee tables and bookshelves

- Generate the "wow" factor

Books are thoughtful gifts that provide a genuine sentiment that other promotional items cannot express. They promote employee discussions and interaction, reinforce an event's meaning or location, and they make a lasting impression. Use your book to say "Thank You" and show people that you care.

The Boomer's Guide to a Worry Free Retirement is available in bulk quantities and in customized versions at special discounts for corporate, institutional, and educational purposes. To learn more please contact our Special Sales team at:

1.866.775.1696 • sales@advantageww.com • www.AdvantageSpecialSales.com

CPSIA information can be obtained at www.ICGtesting.com
Printed in the USA
BVOW08s2054120614

356215BV00023B/172/P